"As a former student leader in my collegiate recovery program, this topic is near and dear to my heart. I know firsthand how hard it is to take that leap of faith into recovery, especially in college where excessive drinking is everywhere. I was honored to share my story with Susan and looked forward to our conversations because it felt like connecting with an old friend--she gets it! I wish I had this book in college, but I'm thrilled Susan captures our stories so that young people understand they're not alone and "hope-rich" is possible…I promise."

Charlotte, from *The Little Book of College Sobriety*

"This book is a groundbreaking glimpse into the ravages and hope of young people overcoming substance use disorders."

Dr. Cara Poland, MD, MEd
Addiction Medicine Specialist

As someone who recognizes how tireless the work is to fight stigma and bring recovery into the light, it has been galvanizing to see Susan's dedication to making this a book not only honoring young people in recovery, but also amplifying their voices--a population that is too often in the shadows."

Dawn Kepler
Collegiate Recovery
Community Coordinator

Other books by Susan Packard

The Little Book
of College Sobriety
LIVING HAPPY, HEALTHY, and FREE

*Stories from
College Students,
a Few Graduates,
and One Mother*

Susan Packard

SIMPLY
GOOD PRESS
EST. 2012

For permission requests, speaking inquiries, and bulk-order purchase options contact: Joyce Ortiz
1jortiz@comcast.net

The Little Book of College Sobriety / Susan Packard

Library of Congress Control Number: 2022908424

ISBN: 978-1-7352585-8-4 (Paperback)
ISBN: 978-1-7352585-9-1 (Ebook)

 Published by Simply Good Press, Montclair, NJ

For Linda

Contents

The Beginning... 9

Why I Wrote this Book.. 10

Terms, Names, Practices.. 11

Introduction 15

One

Who We Are

Chapter One: Our Bodies, Our Brains—and
Always, Our Hearts... 18

    Danni: From High School Valedictorian
       to Prison—One Year Later 20

    Kira: Sober at Eighteen, a Winding Path to Recovery 27

Chapter Two: The Wild Ride of Our Emotions 35

    Sophie: Emotional Turmoil Turns into Strength.................. 36

    Sadie: Social Anxiety almost Destroys Her,
       until College and Recovery... 41

Chapter Three: Our Growing-Up Stories........................ 48

    Ahmed: How Two Adults Change his Life 50

Chapter Four: Prescription Drugs—Proceed
with Caution... 58

    Ted: Prescriptions Can Confuse the Truth........................... 60

Two
How We Gain and Grow Our Sobriety

Chapter Five: A Power Beyond 68
Wyatt: A Light Within, a Power Beyond 70

Chapter Six: Belonging 78
Susan: Beloved Belonging 79

Chapter Seven: Honesty 86
Charlotte: Wanting to Be Perfect 88

Chapter Eight: Me Loving Me 96
Marc: The Year that Changed Everything 97

Three
Living Sober, Stepping Out

Chapter Nine: Graduating 106
Paul: Growing Up Entitled 108
Jordan: Living Two Lives, and One Moment of Clarity 112

Chapter Ten: It's a Family Disease 118
*A Mother's Story: I Gave My Daughter
a Painful Choice* 119

Epilogue 127
Acknowledgements 128
Resources and Contact 130
Discussion and Study Guide 133

The Beginning

Getting sober can be brutal.
But then something happens.
It becomes wonderful.

These are your stories, and a bit of mine too. You are courageous. Lit bright. This book is dedicated to never letting you forget that.

Why I Wrote this Book

I was walking on the campus of my alma mater, Michigan State, one day with my friend Lisa. She works there, and knows I'm in long-term recovery. She turned to me and asked, "Would you like to meet some of the students from the CRC, and say hello?"

I looked at her, perplexed. I had never heard of the CRC.

"Our collegiate recovery community – the CRC,"* she explained. "These are for our students who choose to attend college sober. We can go to their lounge and say hello."

So we went, and in that moment, this book began.

---

* CRCs (Collegiate Recovery Communities) might also be referred to as CRPs, or a similar acronym, depending upon the college. They are communities for students interested in abstaining from drugs and alcohol during college, and engaging in alternative social pursuits.

Terms, Names, Practices

Terms

I know that language matters, because we live with the stigma that surrounds mental health disorders. Healthcare professionals refer to addictions as "substance use disorders," or SUDs. I use the word "addiction" to describe myself before recovery, and some of the storytellers do too, but you don't have to identify with this word. You can substitute "actively using" or "misusing" or another descriptor you're comfortable with.

I sometimes use the term "addiction" as shorthand for substance use disorders and to cover all forms of SUDs, including alcohol and drug use disorders, because I believe the root causes of SUDs are likely the same, whatever substance you're misusing. I use "sober" to include drugs as well as alcohol.

Substance "abuse" is still rampant in our lexicon today, even for national organizations who are trying to help, like SAMSHA, the Substance Abuse and Mental Health Services Administration. The proper word is "misuse." "Abuse" implies we have a choice about being in addiction, and we don't. It's a disorder, or disease.

I often use "rooms of recovery" to mean the actual rooms we gather in for meetings or, more generally, to designate gatherings of sober people.

Names

Some of the names associated with the storytellers throughout this book are pseudonyms to protect anonymity. Some storytellers asked that others read their stories.

Practices

My programs of recovery are Twelve Step–based and deeply steeped in mindfulness and meditation, but I respect any path and I hope that is reflected in this book.

When you own your life,
When you appear,
You become a light by which others can see.
—Greg Boyle

·

Introduction

When we are suffering from substance use disorders, we go missing. We take the back door out and find any means of escape: drugs, alcohol, food, or sex, to name just a few. We do this because of our ferocious inner pain. In the many recovery meetings I've attended, I almost always hear some version of this: "I am unlovable."

Our culture thinks addiction is a failing, but it is really the language of the deeply wounded.

But there's hope on the other side, and it's called Recovery.

Recovery opens up a whole new way of seeing the world. It helps us to stay planted and not run away—to instead be fully present in our lives so we can form our identities, find our voices, and discover all that's true about us. To let the right things define us.

My heartfelt wish is that by hearing these stories, you can touch your own story with tenderness. See how brave you are. Being brave isn't the absence of fear—it's pushing through it to get to the other side.

Your Trek to Recovery

As I listened to each of the storytellers, a shape came together for this book. Their words show the trek that we all take as we journey from addiction into recovery. The stories here, including my own, lay out three parts to our recovery trek:

First, recognizing *how we're made,* and how our growing-up years have formed us.

Second, offering *tools to gain and grow your sobriety* – like sober friends, honesty, openness to spirituality, and starting and ending each day believing in yourself.

Third, *living your recovery* as you stride out into the world, so that you're ready to embrace life, fully alert to its gifts—waiting just for you.

ONE

Who We Are

Chapter One

Our Bodies, Our Brains—and Always, Our Hearts

Sometimes it is necessary to reteach a thing its loveliness.
—Galway Kinnell

The word "disease," commonly used to describe addiction, makes it sound like it's just a matter of our physical bodies. That's not true, and this may be why substance use disorders are so hard for our loved ones to grasp.

They involve every part of us, including how we think, which often seems chaotic, and how we connect with others, which involves our wounded hearts. Then too, there are those holes we feel inside, something a recovery friend of mine named Anne calls our "soul sickness."

Every part of us—body, brain, heart, soul—is part of our disorder.

But our bodies are as good a place to start as any. Our genetics are the DNA we inherit from our ancestors, and they are a key risk factor for addiction. Often, substance use disorders are a multi-generational disease.

This means that if our grandparents or parents or other relatives (but especially our parents) have suffered from addiction, that puts us at a higher risk for it, too.

Let's look at Danni's story. Turn the page.

Danni

From High School Valedictorian to Prison—One Year Later

SCAN TO LISTEN

Growing Up with Suspected Disorders Around Me

I had a pretty typical middle-class upbringing. However, addiction—SUDs, gambling, sex addiction—is common on both sides of my family. I have an uncle on each side who's gotten more DUIs than we can keep track of.

Domestic violence is also common in my mom's family. In my own family, there was some verbal and emotional abuse, and none of us were allowed to raise our voices or show emotion in response to it. My father has never been diagnosed with a substance use disorder, but his alcohol use has caused many problems in my family. I'm not sure that any of this was apparent from the outside. There were never lost jobs or divorce.

Feeling Disconnected

I grew up always feeling disconnected from others. I tried to overcome it through being perfect and pleasing people. It is standard for my father to be very critical, and much of his communication comes in the form of lectures, so I tried avoiding doing anything wrong or that someone would criticize.

In school I joined extracurricular activities to try to feel more connected: marching band, color guard, winter guard, cross country, theater. I graduated high school tied for valedictorian.

A Rape, a Blackout, and Prison

Right before high school graduation, I drank at a party, blacked out, and was raped. I reached out for help from the local health department, and their response was shaming and humiliation. Almost a year later I was at a party and blacked out again. I drove drunk during the blackout and caused a car crash.

I had no memory of what happened. I was told I was airlifted to a hospital. I awoke with two broken legs, a head injury, and learned I had killed someone. So, at nineteen I was a felon and put in prison. I hated myself.

College and Belonging

I had started at a community college before prison, and after I got out, I went back. I eventually finished with an associate degree in human services with a focus on addiction studies. Then I transferred to a four-year university to continue studies in this area and graduated when I was twenty-five.

I think that's why I've made a career in the addiction field, so I can feel connected to others like me, and so I might offer compassion and support to others coming after me. I have had various jobs in this field, and today I'm the coordinator for a university's collegiate recovery community.

I've been looking for belonging all my life, so I could stop feeling so disconnected. But as a young person who got sober at nineteen, I couldn't find a recovery community where I felt like I belonged. Now, because of the work I do today, and the incredibly tight bond I have with the students, I finally feel connected in a big and powerful way, and that enriches my own sobriety, too.

The Bad—and the Good—News about Our Bodies and Hearts

Genetics matter, as in Danni's story. I chose to share her story first because it drives home the physical nature of our disorder. It doesn't matter *how much* we drink. Danni rarely drank. What matters is *how poorly our bodies process alcohol and drugs.*

Danni longed to belong somewhere, which I can relate to, and you might, too. It's common to hear this in the gathering places of recovery. We can really struggle to connect and belong.

I've known Danni for many years, and she has a heart the size of Mount Everest. This past Christmas, I gave her a book about managing life if you're highly empathetic, which she is. Many of us are. These are qualities of the heart.

I wish the experts on SUDs would talk more about the key role our hearts play in keeping us apart, and then later, happily, keeping us connected in recovery. For me, recovery was like coming home to a place I never knew existed.

But our feelings are not "the science," so they get left out by the medical people. The fact is, those I know in recovery have caring, sensitive hearts that often get broken, and in that fragile state, we drink or drug to escape.

That's the bad news about our hearts.

The good news is that eventually, our hearts crack open. In that tender place, we allow someone to reach out their hand, and we take it.

Addiction is isolation, and recovery is connection.

More Good News!

Our hearts are full of goodness, but that can get stuffed down and buried under rejection and shame.

When this happens, pause, take a breath, and treat yourself with loving kindness. Don't ever forget: You are *made good. Unshakably good.*

I wish I had known that earlier in my life, so I pass this truth onto you right now: In this very moment, your heart and soul are shining like the sun.

Do I Really Have SUDs?

If you're wondering whether you have an addiction (SUD), or you just want to confirm you're in the right place reading this book, see if any of these apply to you:

1. I'm never satisfied with one drink or hit. It only begins an endless chain of craving more.
2. I am compulsive and relentless when I want something, whether it's shoes, double-fudge ice cream, or pills. It doesn't matter, I'm all-or-nothing to get it.

3. I keep seeking the high even when the good feelings have disappeared, hoping to get them back.
4. I can be self-destructive when I use drugs and alcohol.
5. I don't fit in, except with the help of alcohol or drugs.
6. I feel like I am too sensitive.
7. I am tortured by loneliness.
8. I am viciously hard on myself.
9. My mind is chaotic. There are far too many thoughts competing for my attention all the time.
10. I feel like I am never enough.
11. I must have been dropped into the wrong family.
12. I try hard to be perfect because I'm sure that if I'm perfect, you will approve of me.

Did you check several? If yes, this might be the right book for you.

Even if you only checked the first descriptor, #1, that could be telling, because #1 captures our universal common ground: When we start, we can't stop.

Our Progress Is Everything

In active addiction, life gets progressively worse. We get sicker and sicker, and we may die. We know many who have. One of the reasons it's so hard to get sober is because we have a disease that tells us we don't have a disease. There's actually a scientific name for this curious state: Anosognosia, the inability to perceive the reality of our condition.

However, the flip side of addiction is true, too: Our sobriety is progressive! The longer we're sober and we keep up our routines of recovery, the better *everything* gets. Progress!

An Instagram post I saw recently said it perfectly:

Addiction is giving up everything for one thing. Recovery is giving up one thing for everything.

Our Overall Mental Health and SUDs

Your overall mental health can also play a role in your SUDs. Like family members with addiction, co-occurring mental health challenges are another marker that indicates a higher risk of addiction. They can appear as anxiety, anorexia, cutting, and depression, among others.

Let's hear Kira's Story.

Kira

Sober at Eighteen, a Winding Path to Recovery

SCAN TO LISTEN

Growing Up, Feeling Worthless

The first time I got drunk I was twelve or thirteen, and I blacked out. Instead of being scared, it felt good to escape, a relief, really, because I was dealing with depression and anxiety. I was like, *My parents drink when they're stressed out, so why not me?* Both of my grandpas are alcoholics, so addiction runs in my family.

Toward the end of middle school, I started talking to high school kids and adults online, Tinder mostly, and meeting up with them. I was hanging around a lot of random people. Some of them smoked weed, so I was probably fourteen when I started smoking weed too, pretty consistently. Sometimes they'd introduce me to new drugs. One time there was cocaine, and I was like, "Oh that's awesome." Another time they had ketamine, and I was like, "Oh that's awesome too."

Suicide Attempts

When I started doing drugs, I began having suicidal thoughts. Because of my depression I used a lot of uppers, and with uppers of course you come down. Sober, I was so down. I knew I was disappointing my family, and I felt worthless. I believed I was a bad person, so I might as well just kill myself. I tried several times. The first time I took a whole bottle of pills. I don't remember it, but I guess I had sixteen seizures, and I had to be put on a ventilator to keep breathing. Even that experience didn't stop me from using again.

Early High School

Before that incident, during the first couple of years of my using, my parents didn't know about it. I snuck out of the house a lot. I did drugs in school, at any point I could. As a high school freshman, I didn't do well academically. Then I got kicked out of that school because now I was selling drugs.

Mid-sophomore year, my family moved to a new school district, which supported my recovery from my mental health problems and substance use disorder. But I was still constantly in and out of rehabs and mental hospitals. For my senior year, the school I was at recommended I move to this amazing alternative school that was more helpful in catering to my needs.

A Fantastic New High School

The new school really helped me. They were very aware of my background. The school offered an IEP, an Individualized Education Program, because of my mental health and substance use disorders. They gave me a designated class time to stress down, to relax, do homework. It wasn't test-based, it was project-based.

I was on and off drugs all through high school, in and out of rehabs, but I started doing well at school because they gave me the emotional and academic support I needed.

Hitting Bottom

I graduated, but I wasn't ready to get sober.

My parents kicked me out, and I was homeless. Toward the end of that using spurt, three or four months, I was supposed to go to college, but I had nothing set up. A week before I was supposed to go, I thought, *How am I going to even do that? I have no books, no money, no car. I'm not prepared at all.*

That's when I finally realized: *I really have a drug problem. I really am an addict.*

I asked my family for help, to send me to a different rehab and halfway house they had heard about nearby, and thankfully they did. It was great. I was in treatment there for three months. My sobriety and spirituality were doing well, but my mental health, not so much, so I used again.

Finally, I went to a treatment center in Illinois mostly focused on mental health, and they got me on correct medications. I haven't used since. My sober date is May 18, 2019.

Starting College Slowly and Thoughtfully

At eighteen, over the summer of 2019, I worked to make money, and I wasn't planning to go to college. I thought I wasn't smart enough, good enough. That I was a drug addict and didn't deserve to go. But my dad said, "Kira, why don't you go to community college and get your brain turning again?"

So I went, took three random classes, and then I realized that I really liked learning! I spent two years there. I wasn't planning to go to a four-year college, for sure not this one I'm at now, because I knew it was so hard to get into. But my parents reminded me that it had always been my dream to go here, so why not just apply to see if I can get in? I had a 3.9 at my community college. I got in!

I went to college in 2021 at twenty years old. I moved there in early summer on purpose, knowing I didn't start school until late August. The extra time allowed me to find a place to live, get acclimated, start slowly. I got work at Whole Foods, started to go to recovery meetings there, and got comfortable being by myself.

Choosing Where to Live

It was hard to figure out where to live at college. I knew I could not be around other people who were using or drinking. Because I was twenty, I didn't have to live on campus, so I got my own apartment.

Today I live alone, and I love it! I hope to live by myself until I graduate. I love having a safe place to come home to.

The Habits Key to Staying Sober

The biggest thing that keeps me sober is the CRC on campus (Collegiate Recovery Community). I don't know what I would do without it. It's not why I came here, but I'm so glad it's here! I plan events for the CRC. We're going to a movie next week, and I'm really excited!

I've also been going to a lot of concerts with another sober friend. And I do cross-stitch a lot. It keeps me busy at home and helps with my anxiety. Also, I Zoom-host a meeting for my home group every week, so I get to see my people there, and that gives me comfort.

My spirituality helps too. I love AA (Alcoholics Anonymous)'s spiritual side, and how it talks about a higher power. My friends in AA know I also go to Buddhist-based recovery meetings and practice Buddhism. I meditate a lot.

Having a set schedule at school and keeping busy with work, school, and my recovery programs are all the things that help keep me sober.

Feeling My Full Self-Worth

I used to hate myself when I was using, but I love myself today. I love who I am. I know I'm a good person.

I love that I'm able to talk about being in recovery, and about my past, and give people who are struggling hope. It's amazing to think about all the opportunities I've gotten, just from sharing my story.

I have light in my life today. I just want to hang out and see what tomorrow brings.

Never Give Up!

What I especially love about Kira's story is that she never gave up on herself. She just *kept trying* to get to a place of balance and peace. I love, too, that she found her goodness. There it was. Right inside her. All along.

To use health language, goodness is our pre-existing condition.

Friends, we have a disorder. We're not to blame for it. We're not bad or weak because of it. Perhaps the examples I can offer from my own life– writing books, and before that, starting new media businesses, like HGTV—suggest that we can be successful even *with* it, when we do the work to get sober.

And we do that by picking up our tools of recovery, like the ones you see here. There's a whole buffet to choose from, and guess what? You can sample options, help yourself to things that work for you, and go back for more of whatever you need, anytime!

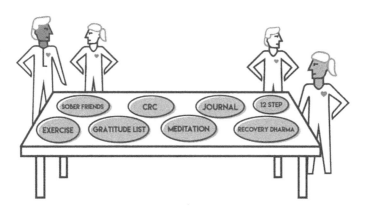

Illustration by *Elisa Vandergriff*

See more buffet items on pages 45 and 117!

Chapter Two

The Wild Ride of Our Emotions

Our tears improve the earth.
—Rumi

I've sat in hundreds of recovery meetings, and when my mind is not cartwheeling and I'm able to listen deeply, I'm convinced that we are more emotional creatures than the average person. We feel too much – or not at all. Our emotions spill out all over the place, or we stuff everything down so we won't feel our feelings at all. Let's listen to Sophie.

Sophie

Emotional Turmoil Turns into Strength

SCAN TO LISTEN

Growing Up Unmoored

I come from a large family with addiction and mental health issues, and my mom always warned me that drugs and alcohol would be very dangerous for me. But I didn't get it. I felt a lot of inner pain starting around twelve or thirteen, and I was deeply unmoored at home. It was a volatile environment, and my parents' marriage was falling apart. I didn't have any coping skills for difficult emotions. Still, I was an academic overachiever, maybe because it was my only means of self-validation.

Between the summer of middle and high school, I grew boobs and started wearing makeup. I was pretty! So going into high school I joined a "popular" group, which I was subsequently kicked out of after my boyfriend broke up with me. From there, I drifted to the less popular, fucked-up kids, basically because they were the only ones who would have me.

I was still driven to get good grades. Sophomore year I made the crew team, and I was introduced to Adderall, which seemed to solve all my problems—it made me feel numb. Not happy, just not miserable. From there, I was always seeking out drugs and alcohol, and I always used alone, mostly because I didn't want anyone else to know that I was using, or how much. It was awful.

College and an Ultimatum

I got into an Ivy League-type university because of my high grades. Going in, I was fueled by stimulants and perfectionism and alcohol, which took the edge off. For a few months I felt like I fit in. I was on the Dean's List my first semester. But I was still using all the time. Then I was raped by a fellow student, and that trauma sped up my downward spiral. My grades—my sole source of self-worth for so long—plummeted, and the university expelled me.

When I came home, my mom said, "I love you very much, but you can't live here. You have two choices: go to rehab or live somewhere else."

So I went to rehab for a whole year. Then I enrolled in a small college in the Southwest, and started living in collegiate recovery housing. It was a lot more structured than a CRC you find on campuses today; we had to live there, attend regular meetings, get therapy, and maintain certain grades.

After nine months in recovery housing, I moved into an apartment with some sober friends. I formed a sober home group, and we had meetings, which was fantastic. Today, I'm in graduate school, working, and six years sober!

This Dream Came True

As far back as sixteen, I never thought I could graduate college clean and sober. But I did! It was one of the proudest moments of my life. It makes me happy to think about it even right now!

In sobriety I've found purpose from the pain, and I'm now working to promote access to treatment and recovery for substance misuse. Today is unimaginably full and hopeful. I love my life now!

The Crash at College

Sophie spoke of having no coping skills for her difficult emotions, so she used substances to take the edge off. College can be liberating and wonderful, but it also brings on the anxieties of navigating a completely new environment and making new friends, along with the stresses of a more challenging course load.

Sophie's using escalated in college. It's a documented fact that being a college student, and living in a campus environment, ratchets up drinking and using. Substance Abuse and Mental Health Services Administration (SAMHSA) research on young adults confirms this. In 2019, 104,000 eighteen-year-old college students met the criteria for an alcohol-use disorder, but among students aged twenty-one, that number doubled to 231,000.

If we are primed for a substance use disorder with factors we looked at in Chapter One, and then add managing our emotions, and throw in the new and pressure-filled environment of college, circumstances are ripe for substance misuse. Experiencing college sober breaks the addiction cycle, when we most need it to!

We All Have Fears

Beneath the impulse to show up as perfect or, really, beneath many emotions such as anger, shame, jealousy, and anxiety, is fear. Fear of not measuring up. Fear of rejection. Fear of trying something and falling flat on your face. Fear is the one emotion I work on relentlessly, because it wants to keep me small.

Recovery, on the other hand, helps us grow bigger than we could have ever imagined. Sadie's story shows us how this can happen.

Sadie

Social Anxiety almost Destroys Her, until College and Recovery

SCAN TO LISTEN

Growing Up Shy

I've always been shy and quiet. I started drinking in middle school because I was always so anxious and because I thought it was fun, at first. In seventh grade my best friend said, "You're an alcoholic!" and I was like, "How can you say that to me?" One time when I was drinking at school my parents found out, and then they sent me to therapy. After that, a lot of the kids hated me, so I found new friends who didn't care if I was drinking and destroying my life.

I started taking Xanax now and then, that my family had. By high school, I was taking Xanax every morning before school and smoking pot every day during lunch hour. I barely graduated high school.

After that I went to our local college because I could get in. In the fall of my freshman year, I overdosed on alcohol and drugs. I was so scared, I detoxed on my own, because I didn't want my parents to know. My roommates took care of me.

The Power of a Sponsor

I knew about NA (Narcotics Anonymous) meetings and so I just drove to one, kind of randomly. I relapsed after that, but I kept going to meetings, and I met a girl there like me, who was young. Except she had four years' sobriety. So I asked her to be my sponsor and she agreed. She's still my sponsor today. I really don't know if I could have gotten sober if I hadn't met her.

Off to the Dream College

After I got sober, that winter break of my freshman year, I had planned to just stay local and go to my college there. But I'd done well enough with my grades in the fall, and had always had a dream of going to my state university, so I applied and was accepted!

My boyfriend was going there, and he was part of its CRC, and he really liked it. I was excited to join, and I've now been a part of it all four years I've been here, including being its student leader. I loved that it gave me a way to find other students in recovery.

Anxiety and depression are super common in early recovery, because the drugs are leaving your system, so the endorphins are low. At our university, if you're with the CRC, you can go to weekly therapy sessions for free. This is a great benefit.

I do think it's hard to *stay* sober in college with just the CRC. You need some structure beyond it, like a sponsor, or Twelve Step meetings, like I go to regularly.

Graduating to a Great New Life

I just received my degree in marketing. I want to do something on the creative side, maybe website design or advertising. I've had fun doing the social media posts for the CRC. My boyfriend graduated, too, and is working, and we're moving in together and that's a big step.

I am at peace with my life today. I have time to do things that I love, like painting and reading books. I also have meaningful relationships with friends and family that I never had before.

I got sober at nineteen, and I'm still sober today, almost five years later. So awesome!

Fear that's Good

Anxiety led Sadie down the dark path of using. After acknowledging her fear, she eventually found peace and balance with the help of recovery groups and a sponsor.

But one kind of fear is very useful: Instinctual fear. It comes when we feel physically unsafe. If we're in circumstances similar to those that caused our original fear, our body remembers for us, and triggers a surge of adrenaline—a warning. We should always pay attention to that, because it helps to keep us safe.

Our Buffet is for *Emotional* Sobriety Too.

There's physical sobriety: Not drinking or drugging each day. And then there's emotional sobriety: Feeling steady, peaceful, and full of joy. None of us will feel all these emotions every day, but we can feel them often enough that we want to keep returning to the buffet!

'

Illustration by *Elisa Vandergriff*

Additional buffet items on pages 34 and 117.

Moving Our Bodies Can Help!

Our bodies carry our emotions, and emotions are simply energy, so it helps to do something with that energy. Taking physical action can allow us to release unsettled emotions. I recently heard in a recovery meeting, "Move a muscle, change a thought." Precisely!

You can take a run or jump on your bike, or head to the gym or to yoga class. Maybe you journal. Perhaps you pray. Or meditate. Every morning, I wake up, have a cup of coffee, then walk upstairs to a room where I light a candle and do centering prayer meditation for twenty minutes. I've been doing this daily for more than ten years. It grounds me, and helps me to stay alert, aware, and fully alive to the day. To not stay small.

Sadie calls her sponsor regularly. She goes to her Twelve Step meetings often, surrounding herself with others who are like her. You can do that, or head over to your CRC lounge to visit with sober friends.

There are hobbies you might love, too. Sadie paints. Kira cross-stitches.

What are some things you do if you're feeling a roller coaster of emotions? (Recovery practices count!) Write them here.

_____

_____

_____

_____

_____

_____

_____

_____

_____

Feel. Deal. Heal.

When you gain some time with physical sobriety, it will become easier to understand and work with your emotions. I promise. You'll learn to feel them, not bury them, and deal with them by sharing them with your therapist or your sober friends. And when you do, those pesky emotions will lose their power over you.

Moving, feeling, dealing, and healing. These are all ways you are taking charge of your life!

A Final Word. It's About Love.

Of all our emotions, the one most steadfast is love. Our mercurial feelings come and go, but love keeps us anchored in what's real, and what's richest.

Always welcome love.

Chapter Three

Our Growing-Up Stories

I am not what happened to me.
I am what I choose to become.
Carl Jung

For some of us, our early years are too painful to dwell on. I get that. Some of the stories I've heard in recovery meetings are so painful, they take my breath away. But it's worth spending a moment to recall your own, before you continue reading here.

Take a moment.

A Part of My Growing- Up Story

My youth wasn't tragic, but I've learned not to minimize its impact on me. As a child, I always felt like I was outside my family circle, looking in. It was like I was invisible to them. I tried to become visible by getting good grades, doing good chores, and helping my little brother. But for many reasons, my parents were laser focused on my two older sisters and baby brother. I was third in line, an unfortunate circumstance of birth order for someone so sensitive.

Getting my mother's attention was nearly impossible, so I'd stage dramatic moments like passing out on the playground in elementary school. It worked. The school nurse would call my mom, and my mom would come and take me home. With just me there, she gave me the attention I yearned for.

What All Kids Need

As children, we should be nurtured and made to feel secure. This reassurance should come in the form of unconditional love from the adults in our lives. If we know we're loved, and that the big people have our backs, we come to believe in our own basic goodness.

In a world that makes sense, children shouldn't have to do anything to be loved. They shouldn't have to perform, prostrate themselves, or become a drama princess on the playground to be loved.

And most certainly, in a world that makes sense, parents shouldn't abandon their children, like Ahmed's did.

Ahmed

How Two Adults Change his Life

SCAN TO LISTEN

Growing Up with Seared Memories

I'm a first-generation American. My parents came here from Egypt. You never know what "normal" growing up is until you're grown up. One of the first memories that's seared in my mind is coming home from a weekend visitation with my dad—my parents divorced when I was two or three—and seeing all our belongings in front of the house, because my mom, sister, and I were being evicted.

We lived in a homeless shelter for a time, when I was between three and four. My mother had a mental health disorder, and her brothers came here to the United States and brought her back to Egypt. The weird thing is they decided to leave me and my sister here.

My sister and I were in foster care, but then my dad and his new wife got custody of us. Things were okay for a while. But when I was twelve, my dad planned this trip to Egypt. It's another one of those moments seared into my brain. I remember dropping him off at the bus station to go to the airport, and I was crying so hard, and no one understood why. I knew he'd never come back. And I was right. He never came back.

My Disease Starts and Worsens through High School

We then lived with my stepmom, and at thirteen or fourteen I started drinking. I didn't really like it, but I liked that it helped me become sociable. My disease was progressing. I was drinking and using drugs weekly—weed, Oxycontin, ecstasy. By sophomore year it became a daily routine. I was smoking weed almost every hour of the day. Because of all that I had to repeat my senior year of high school. Then I was arrested on a felony charge of possession with intent, but luckily got probation.

The World Comes Crashing Down

I squeaked by the next three years, still using. But then my girlfriend got pregnant. I thought, *Why not go to college and get rich, so all my problems would be over?*

But due to my criminal record, I had to complete a treatment program to qualify for student financial aid. I couldn't afford college without it. I figured I'd check the box and go to rehab, but I had no intention of quitting drugs and alcohol. I did, however, want to be a dad to my newborn son, unlike what my dad was to me.

So I found a treatment program and went, but I wouldn't call myself an alcoholic or addict in the treatment groups. In fact I would openly fight with others, saying that I wasn't one.

Life Changes, Thanks to Two Men

I met Ron, who worked at the treatment center and was my counselor. He said, "Look, you signed up for treatment because you want something from us. What do you want from us?" And I told him I just needed to finish the program so I could get a loan and go to college.

So Ron said, "If you want to complete this you can't miss any more sessions. And I need you to go to one Twelve Step meeting and come back and tell me about it." He didn't say go to ninety meetings in ninety days like you hear in the rooms; he said one. I feel like he saved my life because he made it possible for me to take the next step.

I went to the meeting, and I met a man named Daniel. He was so kind. He made me feel welcome. He gave me his phone number. Then he gave me a book and told me to read certain parts of it and to call him after I did. Daniel would eventually become my sponsor. Two weeks after that first meeting, I stopped fighting my disease. I went to another meeting, and Daniel was there, and that's when my recovery started. I got sober at twenty-two.

Finding a Sober Community in College and Beyond

I started college, and as an undergrad I joined the collegiate recovery community there. I owe so much to them. I truly don't believe I would have the life I have today without that support. Nothing can replace the lifelong friends and mentors I made during that time, who understood what it was like to navigate life as a young person in recovery. A sort of Fraternity for the Sunlight of the Spirit.

The ability to stay sober during undergrad, with support from the CRC, motivated me to become a graduate student too. While working at a collegiate recovery community after I graduated, I received my master's degree in social work. Today I work in the Office of Student Life and Wellness at a large university, and I'm surrounded by students who are just like me, trying to balance recovery, school, work, and life. They are so incredibly inspiring, and they help to keep me sober every day, along with my Twelve Step recovery practices.

Understanding the Power of Recovery

Today I understand what the power of recovery is. And I understand that while I can't control a lot of things, there are things I can do to be in control of my life. I can continue my professional work and maybe make a difference, and I can keep up my recovery work by going to meetings and helping and sponsoring other young men.

Ron and Daniel gently guided me to begin walking this path, toward the incredible life I have today. Maybe I can be the adult that helps a young man, like they helped me. At the very least, I will have the opportunity to be the father my two boys deserve.

Adverse Childhood Experiences (ACEs)

Ahmed had multiple traumas growing up: Physical neglect, emotional neglect, a parent with mental illness, and abandonment. The Centers for Disease Control and Prevention, or CDC, call such traumas "adverse childhood experiences" (ACEs). You may have already heard this term if you went to rehab. If you have had several of these experiences, you're at a much higher risk for mental health challenges, including substance misuse. You can google "What are the 10 ACEs of Trauma?" and compare it to your growing-up years.

Who is Your Champion?

The beautiful part of Ahmed's story, to me, is that he had two adults in his life who gently guided him in recovery. I call people like these our "champions." In Chapter Eight, you'll hear from Marc, who has a champion in Victor. Do you have an adult in your life like that? How about friends or relatives?

Take a moment to list the champions that have helped you get sober, or those in your life today.

_____

_____

_____

How About My Family? It Was Normal!

In the next chapter you'll hear from Wyatt, who describes his childhood as loving, and in Chapter Seven, Charlotte says much the same thing. They had no adverse childhood experiences that contributed to their misuse. Perhaps you didn't, either.

It can quite simply come back to how we are made: Our temperaments, genetic ancestry, and our tolerance for risk. Peer pressure is another factor.

In short, we can have SUDs without any childhood trauma. But from the stories I hear in the rooms of recovery, childhood traumas can play an enormous, heartbreaking role.

Chapter Four

Prescription Drugs—Proceed with Caution

No pessimist ever discovered the secrets
Of the stars, or sailed to an unchartered land,
Or opened a new heaven to the human spirit.
Helen Keller

This chapter is about a thorny issue. I hesitated including it because the right answer for one person may be wrong for another. But it's an important issue on college campuses today, so here goes.

This chapter is about taking prescribed medicines for our mental health, and understanding when the routine of taking them for our health slips into taking them to escape.

For those of us with SUDs and no other co-occurring disorder, it's about how we can, too easily, find and misuse prescription drugs.

Legitimate Use or Not?

In the early 2000s, deaths from opioid overdoses were mounting. The war on prescription drugs—and doctors too loosely prescribing them—had begun in earnest. As the years went on, the use of controlled medications for non-medicinal use began tearing families apart. Loved ones overdosed, workplace costs skyrocketed due to absenteeism and employee turnover, and college students found the drugs readily available, even without prescriptions.

In a study of college students, over 33 percent said it was easy to get prescriptions for pain medications, and 44%—almost half—said it was easy to get prescriptions for sedatives.* One student I talked with said, "It's crazy easy to get pills on campus." Many of these pills are now being laced with fentanyl, and campus deaths are on the rise.

Many of us legitimately need medicines for our mental health, and if we do, we need to take them, much as we'd take a prescribed antibiotic for a physical ailment like strep throat. But sometimes taking these medications can confuse and mask an SUD. Here's Ted's story.

---

http://hecaod.osu.edu/podcast/college-prescription-drug-study/

Ted

Prescriptions Can Confuse the Truth

SCAN TO LISTEN

Growing Up an Aspiring Astronaut

I always wanted to be an astronaut growing up. Probably lots of kids do, but I never grew out of that. I recall going to space camp in Huntsville in fifth grade, and I got to be captain of the space shuttle – and I saw how massive the rockets were. It was amazing.

In middle school, my parents divorced, and it wasn't a friendly divorce. I became kind of withdrawn and started having depression and anxiety.

Adderall Becomes a Gateway to Misuse

I have ADHD, so in high school I was prescribed Adderall. I saw it not as a drug but as a necessary prescription. But it turned from *this is a helpful tool* to *I can use this to have fun!* Abusing Adderall was the start of my using. I took it in the morning before class, which was how it was prescribed, but I would also take it to stay up at night and play video games. It was maybe mild abuse, but it got worse.

College: Addicted to Anything Mind-Altering

I know now that my SUD kicked up when I was a freshman in college. I wanted to be more social and outgoing, so by second semester I started to drink a lot and go to parties. I failed a couple of classes, which had never happened in high school.

That would begin seven years of being in and out of college, going to rehabs, taking time off from school because I was failing, and once, taking a medical leave. During those seven years, I drank, took Adderall, Xanax, and Valium, and I smoked weed. Basically, I was addicted to anything that was mind-altering.

I got sober three times in that span of years, but it never stuck. There is no shortage of pills around college campuses, but I was never in a position where I needed to seek them out, because I had prescriptions for them all.

I Don't Have a Substance Use Problem!

For the longest time I didn't believe I had a substance use issue. I just thought I had mental health challenges and that the pills and drinks would quiet them. I fooled myself for a long time thinking that, because the pills I was taking were prescribed, they must be "safe."

At times I stopped drinking, sure that *that* was the problem. So I'd quit alcohol, but then the pills or smoking weed would ratchet up. For a time, I was just smoking weed, because I thought it was harmless, but I ended up relapsing and using alcohol and drugs again, wanting more of an escape than weed could give me.

When I withdrew medically from the university for a semester because I was failing classes, I still didn't think I had a substance use problem. I just thought I was depressed.

Hitting Rock Bottom

In January of 2021, I was going to school online and living at home. That was during COVID. There I used mainly weed. That summer, I went to a music festival with some friends and had a complete relapse. On the night of August 28, I got so drunk at a bar I blacked out. I don't remember, but I guess I went back to my cousin's place, and he helped me take a shower. I do recall lying on his bathroom floor, feeling like I was going to die, and I didn't care.

That was rock bottom for me. I haven't had pills or a drink or weed since. My sober date is August 29, 2021.

How I Keep Sober Today

I went back to campus and aggressively sought out recovery meetings and found an NA meeting that I still go to today. I tried AA, but I like NA better. I instantly felt like I belonged at NA, and it helped me to see that I did have a drug problem, not just an alcohol-use issue. I couldn't deny any longer that even though the prescriptions I got from doctors were "legitimate," they were hiding my disorder, not helping it.

My sober practices today are going to the CRC events, their All-Recovery meeting each week, my NA weekly meeting, and I also participate in SOAR, the student-led social organization that was around before our CRC was developed. SOAR stands for Spartans' Organization for All Recovery.

I decided to move into recovery housing, too. It's a really supportive environment. It feels good to have a community there. We have our own meetings every week, and I've made new friends.

What Today Feels Like

I'm so glad to be here. So glad I didn't die that night in August, when I couldn't have cared less about living anymore.

I'm happier now, more content with my life. It was so ironic, but using my own prescription drugs didn't help. Instead they *exacerbated* my mental health problems—I was unhappy so I'd take the pills, but they ended up making me more unhappy.

I'm not so worried what people think anymore. I used to feel self-conscious about taking this much time to get through college, but I don't worry about that anymore.

Final Thoughts on Adderall, and Life

I'm off my Adderall completely, and sometimes paying attention in school is hard, but my sobriety is more important than my ADHD. I choose sobriety as the best life for me.

I'm graduating in a month with a degree in Astrophysics, and maybe I will become an astronaut, or be the one who discovers life on other planets. Who knows? I'm sober and free and today is good.

Caring for Our Mental Health

Our mental health is as important as our physical health. We need to care for it and our doctors can help with that. Each person's management of their overall mental health is personal to them, and in the end, only you and your doctor can know the right course. Having SUD adds a layer of complexity, so it should be factored into your overall care.

There are no easy answers here, but I offer this chapter as one brave young man's journey to clarity.

TWO

How We Gain and Grow Our Sobriety

Chapter Five

A Power Beyond

Once you know the God of love,
you fire all the other gods.
—Mirabai Starr

There is something within us that's always moving, growing, dancing. Something bigger than you could imagine. It's in each of us, and this is our spiritual dimension of self. It exists just like our bodies, the physical dimension of ourselves.

What's baffling and powerful (to use a couple of AA words) is that our spirituality is inside us, but it's also much bigger than us. It's a mystery in that way, a paradox; two things that seem contradictory but can simultaneously be true.

What's inside me I call my "goodness," and the bigger-than-me part I choose to call God. You might have a different name. You might call both Love. Or Divine Spark. Or Great Mystery. The names don't matter. What matters is your spiritual sobriety—yet another form of sobriety—and developing it in recovery, if you feel moved to do so.

We need to heal more than our bodies and brains in recovery, as we discussed in Chapter One. We need to heal our rampant state of disconnection, that soul sickness, by reaching for the sunlight of spiritual connection.

When we reach for something bigger than us, we feel less alone. And we become avatars of love.

Wyatt's story illuminates this.

Wyatt

A Light Within, a Power Beyond

SCAN TO LISTEN

Growing Up Loving Music

I had a great childhood. As a young kid, I knew I wanted to play music. I was beating on pots and pans playing drums at three years old, which led to my mother signing me up for piano lessons in second grade. In fifth grade I learned bass trombone, and my middle school band director asked me to play for a new CD he was recording, so I did. I was twelve years old at the time. We performed at Sheldon Concert Hall in St. Louis, Missouri. During that performance it hit me: I knew that I wanted to play and perform music for the rest of my life.

Danger Signs

I got drunk the first time I drank, at fourteen. I was on a golf course with some of my dad's friends, and they gave me beers. I was drinking on and off for the next two years, and at seventeen, I started drinking heavily and began smoking pot.

I thought then I might have a problem, but I kept making excuses because I didn't want to stop. My cousin is a heroin and fentanyl addict, and when my parents worried about me I'd say, "Don't worry about it, I'm not like my cousin."

Ratcheting Up Drinking and Using in College

In college it all ratcheted up for three straight years. I was doing cocaine, Adderall, Xanax, psychedelics, drinking, and smoking pot. Toward the end of my using, I overdosed on Xanax—I didn't know it was pressed with fentanyl.

Everything went wrong. I hated myself. I started losing everything that mattered. My relationships were terrible, my home life was awful, and eventually it got to the point where I genuinely didn't want to play music anymore. It was the most incredibly dark and lonely place.

I had a psychotic break when I went home in May of my junior year. I told my parents I was done with music, that I was going to sell all my instruments and drop school. I screamed at them, "I want to stop living! I don't want to do this anymore!"

My parents said, "You can keep living the way you are, and move out of this house, or you can go to treatment." So I went.

Going to Treatment

I went to a treatment program in Southern California. You know how you get that feeling in your soul that *this feels right*? I said to myself, "This will be okay."

They had AA meetings there. I remembered when I was seventeen, and my parents took me to an AA meeting, and I didn't want to go. Back then at that meeting, some random older guy came up to me and said, "Let me give you a hug!" and I was like, *I don't know you. Stay away from me.*

But I guess I was finally ready in treatment, so I went to an AA meeting. I was in a room full of strangers explaining so well all the things I was feeling that I hadn't told anyone before. So I was willing to give AA a shot. That's the program I still practice.

Stepping Out into the World

I was in treatment a little over two months. I was planning on staying there a full ninety days, but I got a call from a friend who asked me if I wanted to participate in this college program in Aspen, Colorado, playing with Christian McBride. He's a living legend! He's played with some of the most influential musicians to ever live, including James Brown, and he's won a lot of Grammys. So I was incredibly grateful to accept the offer and went to do that for two weeks.

It was a great test for going back to college because I was with people who used, and I didn't want to. That was so beautiful.

Where To Live, What To Do

When I was in treatment, trying to figure out where I would live when I went back to school, my mom discovered there was a CRC at my college. I had no idea. I thought it was amazing that they had this community!

Then I found out they had recovery housing too, and I thought it would be good to live there my first year in sobriety. That's where I live now.

The people who live here and are a part of the CRC make living in sober housing great. It's kind of interesting though, we get freshmen whose parents just tell them they have to live on the sober floor, whether they want to or not. But they're not in recovery. So some people use here.

It's not perfect, but it's a great opportunity to practice living life on life's terms, meaning there are things we just can't control. Staff recently had a meeting about it, and things are better. We have a recovery housing specialist on the floor here who helps us, and she's incredible, really helpful.

The Power to Stay Sober

The main thing that keeps me sober is my relationship with my Higher Power, whom I choose to call God. And I actively practice gratitude for any situation in life, whether it's good or bad. Also, AA's program is amazing. I keep in touch regularly with my sponsor, and I still attend my home meetings because they happen on Zoom.

The CRC has been a big part of this, too. They offer free weekly therapy sessions, which is amazing, and I get to hang out with people who take their recovery seriously and want to live this way. That's pretty great.

The CRC events we get to go to together are so much fun, like tailgates and horseback riding. For Thanksgiving we're getting together for "Friendsgiving," and that will be awesome. Things I would have never done when I used, because then, I just wanted to isolate.

Self-Acceptance is a Promise Come True

I have fun today just sticking to the basics, like listening to and playing music. I feel more in touch with myself when I'm playing music.

I used to tell myself these awful things about who I was. I would just pray every night that I wouldn't wake up. It was so dark. But today it's so beautiful, I *want* to wake up. I've never had this level of self-acceptance that I have today. I haven't felt this happy before in my life.

"Stop Worrying."

Wyatt said that in those dark moments, which we've all had in active addiction, he hated himself. Here's the thing—God never knows what we're talking about when we judge ourselves unworthy, or unlovable.

The God I know, and I suspect Wyatt knows too, could never be disappointed with anything we do. Sad perhaps, but never disappointed. Instead, I'm convinced we would hear, "Stop worrying about 'doing good,' and just keep remembering, you *are* good."

The Spiritual Path that Suits You is the Right One

It's hard to talk about our spiritual path because it's such a personal thing. It's hard, too, because words are limiting, and the God I know, and I hope you know too, can't be bound by one idea, theology, or religion. This God is as big as the ocean.

Just like there's no one right path to recovery, there's no one right path to explore your spirituality; many paths can lead you there. Gazing up at a sea of stars. Meditating. Feeling the sun on your face. Hiking in the mountains. Kneeling in prayer. Doing something nice for someone when they least expect you to.

Let Some Music Flow

We worshiped alcohol and drugs for a time, and they left us empty and alone. I believe that when we get sober and our bodies are free from the toxins of our addictions, we can feel the holes inside us. Everyone has holes, and that's okay because we're human. Slowly, God heals these holes, and if we could see it happening, we'd see billions of them filling with light.

Let some of that sweet music flow through you.

Chapter Six

Belonging

To bring ourselves to others
makes the whole world less lonely.
—Mary Karr

In recovery rooms, we often express feelings of not belonging anywhere. It's that chronic state of disconnect, or soul sickness that we feel in active addiction.

That was the biggest driver of my using. Sheer and utter loneliness, although I was happily married and starting a family. It wasn't rational, but it was real. I got sober because I found a community where they understood how I was cratering inside. Where I heard my story in theirs.

Here's mine.

Susan

Beloved Belonging

SCAN TO LISTEN

Growing Up Sensitive

I grew up as a sensitive girl, shy and easily hurt by my sisters, brother, and mother. My dad was wonderful but he worked hard and I didn't see him as much. I loved to write and started journaling in eighth grade, and I still have that diary. Those passages reflect a girl alone in a home with many big personalities, trying to figure out where she fit.

I took my first drink at fourteen. I was with three girl-friends, and one knew two guys from Germany who were brothers: Fritz and Hans. Fritz was old enough to buy beer. And to drive, which was kind of key. As Fritz ran into the beer store that first night I drank, Hans announced that he would let each of us kiss him. Like he was some gift. He was maybe fifteen. So while Fritz drove, each of us took a turn. Believe me, he was no gift.

Fritz bought each of us a GIQ of Pabst. GIQ stood for Grand Imperial Quart. Beer brewers don't bottle in GIQs anymore, maybe because it's easy to become an alcoholic after a couple of those. So my first drink was a quart of beer, which is 32 ounces. I really liked how it felt, like I belonged to a group and would be accepted. Over my remaining high school years, my girlfriends and I added pot and sometimes pills, like MDMA. I know now that we were taking Ecstasy, but we called it MDMA.

None of this affected my honor roll grades, and somehow, I hid it all from my parents. I don't recall ever being grounded in high school.

College

I went to a state university where a lot of my family had gone. Before I finished my freshman year, I quit college, and, no surprise, my parents were not happy. It was the first bold thing I'd done in my life. It just felt vital for me to move away from my school, home, and parents before something really dire would happen to me, but I didn't know what that was. I'd been drinking a lot all freshman year and taking speed to get through studying. Speed back then is meth today, another startling truth.

I moved to San Diego, and to pay bills I took a job waitressing on the graveyard shift, midnight to six. Two important things happened during my time there. First, I lost my virginity, which was a relief, but why I needed to go two thousand miles to lose it, I haven't a clue. Second, I realized I was a terrible waitress.

I went back to college after being away two semesters, and I wish I could say I stopped using, but that wouldn't be true. I drank heavily, took speed to study, and once I tried LSD. It was terrifying. I remember spending most of the night throwing up on the front lawn of my dorm, and crying inside, *When will this be over?*

Had there been a collegiate recovery community back then, I might have known what questions to begin asking myself, or where to go when I thought I was losing my mind.

Still, I graduated from the honors college of my university. Grades validated my "being normal," I guess. If I could pull good grades, nothing could really be wrong with me.

The Working World

I consider myself very lucky, because I sort of stumbled into an industry as it was just taking off. Yes I worked very hard and had a decent brain, but luck played a role too, which it does for most people who achieve things in life, if they're honest with you. Some say you make your own luck. That might be partly true. I helped to build the multichannel media industry, and it was exciting.

The first time I really thought I had a problem with alcohol, I was twenty-six, living in Dallas for HBO. I began the habit of stopping by the wine store on my way home from work almost every night, and buying a bottle of wine. Some nights I'd drink one or two glasses, some nights the whole bottle. The need for that stop every night—the distress I might *run out*, troubled me, and slowly I began to pay attention to my drinking.

I was assaulted in a hotel room traveling for work in my late twenties, and stopped trusting anyone I worked with. It's remarkable how you can be "successful" without trusting a soul.

My disease progressed, and by then I was married and we had a young son. I remember thinking, *When he gets old enough that he'll notice, I'll stop my nightly drinking.* That never happened.

There's a moment in time when you make a choice, and your life veers in a new direction because of it. For me that choice was joining HGTV. There I met a group of people, and especially my boss, whom I could trust. It was in this job that I began to take the slow painful steps toward sobriety.

Beloved Belonging

In my career as a woman leader, we often talk about "getting a seat at the table", which means being at a high enough level in an organization, where you can impact change. This table seats only a few.

When I entered recovery, I found a table that seats everyone. I found people who didn't ever seem to give up on me. There were six women who, from day one, surrounded me with their spines of steel and their fierce hearts. Many years later, they are still my best friends. I could call any of them at 2 a.m. and say, "I'm scared," and they'd be ringing my doorbell.

They told me I was not alone until I finally believed it. They told me I was not in charge, and I came to know a God who loves me, no matter what.

As I meditate each morning on the wonder of my life today, I now think of God as *We*. Not He, or She. God is We.

Who are your close recovery friends?

Write them here, and describe why you care about them.

_____

_____

_____

_____

_____

_____

_____

_____

_____

_____

_____

_____

_____

_____

_____

_____

Safe at Last

For those of us with substance use disorders, it's important that we find communities where we feel safe, because then we can begin to hear our real voice–the one that despairs and longs and hopes there is hope, all in the same breath. This is how we form our identities and come to know our true selves.

I laugh and sometimes think that we're like one of the wandering African rhinos, who grows up separated from their herd. They are always endangered until they can find a herd that takes them in, then they become safe. That's what recovery has been for me, except for being a rhino. (Although for many wandering years, I was a wino).

Our disorder tells us that we're separate from everyone else and the only friends we need are drugs and alcohol. But that's a lie. You either walk toward love or away from it. With substance use disorders, our solution is each other.

Chapter Seven

Honesty

*If you tell the truth, you don't have
to remember anything.*
—Mark Twain

Lies are exhausting. At least they were for me when I was
in active addiction. How do you keep track of them all?
Who you told what? And what if *all these people were in
the same room at the same time?* Terrifying.

Honesty is a big topic in recovery meetings because
we've seen how easy it has been for us to "modify" the
truth. Especially the truths we tell ourselves. To maintain
a healthy recovery, we've learned that telling the truth is
a bit part of feeling happy, healthy and free.

In a recent meeting, a friend of mine who is pretty
consistently hilarious, said that recovery has ruined her
ability to lie. "I can't even lie anymore about being late!
I used to say that I got stuck in traffic, and I want to
say that so badly now! And I think, *It's just a little lie, it
doesn't matter*! And then I think, *No, it's all that matters.*"

When you tell the truth, you may initially feel a little afterburn, but over time? You feel your worth.

Our Secrets Keep Us Sick

The *real story,* what is actually true about us that we hide from others, becomes our secret, and our secrets keep us sick. We've stuffed them down to the deepest parts of our souls, locked in, cradled tight, and they build up over time, like a pressure cooker. When you're filled with them, there's no space for the light to get in. But as you free them, by becoming open and honest, there's room for all your goodness to breathe.

Here's Charlotte's story. For her, a moment of truth changed everything.

Charlotte

Wanting to Be Perfect

SCAN TO LISTEN

Growing Up Living for Everyone but Me

I started drinking in the ninth grade, and it was pretty much off to the races. I didn't really have any issues growing up, but I was always wanting to be perfect at everything. I found that alcohol quieted my mind.

When I first blacked out, I was at a small New Year's Eve parade my hometown has every year, and my friend had a handle of Southern Comfort. My older brothers saw me there and called my parents to pick me up. I was frightened and embarrassed and stunned by the effects alcohol had on me. My parents put me on lockdown and took my cell phone away. In a way I was relieved. I felt so much shame.

But I didn't stop. By my junior and senior years of high school, my drinking had become really bad. I was just incredibly lost—it was like feeling soul sick. I had been living for everyone except me. When I drank, I wasn't so driven to impress other people and to be the best at everything.

Off to College, Off to Rehab

I got into a prestigious university. I kept pushing myself to get good grades and my drinking really ratcheted up, because I put all this stress on myself. I had a great group of friends who were worried enough about me that they called my parents. It wasn't one single event, just a collection of bad nights where they'd have to carry me home or wonder where I was that night. Part of me breathed a sigh of relief. I knew I couldn't keep living like this, but I didn't know how to change.

I left college, and for the next two years, while I stayed out, I relapsed again and again. I was in and out of rehabs, going for everyone but me. I'd sit there listening to other people and think, *These people don't know me. They don't know my life.*

After two years of trying just about everything to get sober and failing, I was finally exhausted enough, and willing enough, to do anything. Up until this point, I'd thought I could leave school, get sober, and go back to my old life—that I had it all under control. But these were all lies I was telling myself.

One Honest Moment Changed Everything

The transformation in me happened when I was finally gut-wrenchingly honest with myself about my life. I could finally get sober when I accepted the truth-that I had a disease-and I no longer kept my challenges with sobriety from my friends and family. I'd been trying to do this alone for so long. Now I knew I needed to start leaning on people who cared about me. I really started to build a life and my own identity when I finally stopped hiding the truth from myself and everyone else.

Setting Myself Up to Succeed

At twenty-four, I was ready to go back to my university. They say in some recovery programs that "you're ready when you're ready," and that was certainly true for me. I set up my college environment so I would have structure and reinforcements around me. I did some research about the university and learned it had a collegiate recovery community, so I called someone in the program and made my first connection.

It was scary going back. The CRC helped me make new friends and integrate into a new community. I'd been there before, but not sober. Before I left, I'd barely learned how the university worked, and all my friends had now graduated. The CRC provided me with friendships and support, and made me feel welcome.

Proudly Wearing My Recovery

I knew I could help other students struggling with sobriety. I became the CRC's student leader and lent a hand, sharing my story, organizing social events, leading weekly meetings, and giving people rides.

Most important, I mentored younger students with zero days, five hours, or one week sober, who were going through the same things I had gone through two years prior.

I wore a recovery sash on graduation day. I'm very proud of how I left college. I still keep up with my CRC friends. They helped me to be brave and to get to the finish line there.

True to Myself Today

I've been sober over three years now. The word "disease"—having the disease of alcoholism—isn't a heavy word for me today. I accept it as a part of who I am, but not the most important part.

Now, out of college, I'm working full-time and I love my work routine. I go to bed at a reasonable hour, wake up early, drink coffee, go to the gym, and make time for meditation/prayer/gratitude. I've realized, now that I'm out of college, how physical health and mental health are inextricably linked.

My awareness continues to evolve. Problems of everyday life do crop up. I initiated a breakup with my boyfriend because I had the feeling we weren't right for each other, and couldn't ignore it any longer. He's an incredible person and did absolutely nothing wrong. I started seeing a therapist for three months post-breakup to process my emotions. I also went to more recovery meetings during that time.

Life happens, but I love my life today. I have a good career, amazing friends, and a rock-solid family. And I love myself, too. I love my own version of myself, no one else's. It's who I always was, but it had gotten hidden behind alcohol and my perfectionism. Alcohol covered up all the good inside me, which I can let shine today.

Accepting Our Truth

Maybe our hardest truth is accepting we have a disease called addiction. We fight and claw our way around that truth, until one desperate day, we stop fighting. Many rooms of recovery call this our moment of surrender. I personally hate the word surrender because it sounds like we've *lost.* The opposite is true in recovery, we've *gained* our lives back. We own ourselves again, like Charlotte does.

Perfectionism is Crippling

Like Danni in Chapter One, and Sophie in Chapter Two, Charlotte was driven to be perfect. So many of us with SUDs grow up feeling "less than," so, being perfect becomes our compulsive response. Perfect grades. Perfect on social media. Perfectly put together on the outside, when inside we are cratering.

I don't know where we got it in our heads that we had to be perfect. No one else is, so why us? Other people are as messed up as we are—they just have their own stories. Perfectionism is crippling. It sucks all the joy out of life. I'd much rather have a friend who's real than one who's perfect.

The author John Green said: "I don't know a perfect person. I only know flawed people who are still worth loving."

YOU are worth loving.

Sober Friends Can Call You on Your Bullshit

When our thinking gets distorted and dishonest, our sober friends, sponsors, and allies can help. Here's an example:

Sponsor Chase: "Hey Jim, what'd you do last night?"

Sober Jim: "Some guys and I met at a frat party. There was alcohol everywhere, but I didn't even *think* of drinking!"

Chase: "What kind of alcohol?"

Jim: "Beer, tequila, Jack Daniels, and oh, I saw a handle of Smirnoff too. Some of the guys were doing shots of Jack!"

Chase: "How many shots?"

Jim: "Well I counted one guy that did four!"

Pause

Chase: "You counted?"

Jim: "Well, yeah …"

Chase: "Do you think a party like that's good for your sobriety?"

Jim: "Um, maybe we should talk about it a little more."

Chase: "How about now?"

Living with Integrity, True to You

The moment we accept the whole truth—first, that we have a substance use disorder, and then, that it touches all parts of us–our bodies, our thinking, and our hearts and souls, too—that's when we start living as a whole, undivided person. These truths are one important form of "living with integrity".

Remember learning about whole numbers in grade school? Whole numbers are also called integers, a word with the same Latin root as integrity. They're whole because they can't be made into fractions, or split apart. Living with integrity is when we "integrate" (another related word) our truth and live in peace with it.

Being honest and true to ourselves helps us make good life choices, like, *Is this the job I really want?* Or, *Is this the right romantic partner?* Sometimes these decisions are hard. Charlotte's decision to separate from her boyfriend came from something inside her, an inner voice that she couldn't ignore any longer. That's integrity: Making honest choices that are true to you. Even when it's hard.

Even if it means telling someone you're late because of *you,* not the traffic.

Chapter Eight

Me Loving Me

*Hardships often prepare ordinary
people for an extraordinary destiny.*
—C.S. Lewis

The road from addiction to recovery is transformative.
As we stay sober, the drugs and alcohol leave our bodies
and we start feeling better, our thinking becomes clearer,
and our hearts begin opening, if only a crack.

It might be, however, that the biggest transformation
of all comes when we toss out self-loathing, and replace
it with self-love. You loving you. *This is a crucial step in
your recovery, especially as a young adult.* With a solid
foundation of self-worth, you can do anything! Like
Marc, who went from having a criminal record of nine
convictions, to the leader he is today.

Marc

The Year that Changed Everything

SCAN TO LISTEN

Growing Up, the Arrests Mount

I'm a third-generation Hispanic male and second-generation college student. My mother is one of the few people in our large extended family, before me, to pursue higher education. My parents have been married over thirty years, and I have one older brother. I had fewer restrictions than my older brother growing up.

The first time I drank was at a Quinceañera, which is a celebration for a Hispanic girl turning fifteen. I was fourteen at the time, and there were unattended coolers everywhere. Somebody handed me a 16-ounce Budweiser and I drank the whole thing. It felt good, and the kids thought I was cool. I liked that and wanted to be a part of their group.

2017 was a Big Year

After that first time with the Budweiser, any time there was alcohol available, I'd be sure I was there. Once I got a car, it was a lot easier to drink. I pretty much drank all the time after that.

I had a daughter when I was a teenager. When her mother and I separated, I spiraled into deep alcoholism and addictions. The next few years were awful, leading up to 2017. By then I had nine convictions on my record: Two DUIs, unlawful carrying of a weapon, a couple assaults. Thankfully, they were all misdemeanors. One night I blacked out and trashed my car and woke up the next morning in the drunk tank.

That morning, I was told that the local police were there the night before, and they wanted to arrest me for all these offenses. But apparently a state trooper showed up and asserted his authority over the locals. He must have had some understanding of addiction when he saw me. He said the arrest would only be a bench warrant for noncompliance in court.

I didn't have a Higher Power then, but today I see that as a God moment, because it was then, sitting in jail, with that trooper's gift of grace, when I finally accepted who I was. That I had a disease, and I needed to treat it.

Walking Home

I walked home from jail because my car had been trashed and I told my parents I needed to go to rehab. We found a place but it cost $5,000 plus my dad's insurance. It took us twelve days to raise $5,000, so I detoxed on their couch which was really scary, and dangerous. Then I went to rehab.

Toward the end of those four weeks of rehab, I developed a relationship with a Higher Power. My rehab counselor Victor also became very important to me. He *told* me, didn't ask, but *told* me I was to go to a sober-living home for three months, then I was to go to college, and then I would have a good life.

So I went to a men's sober-living place, and began giving back to recovery in many ways, including taking meetings into treatment centers. In the fall, I applied to the big university that was near the sober-living home. I found out they also had a collegiate recovery program, and that I needed to apply for that too, so I did.

My Recovery Gained Me Admission to College

The university declined my application. But on December 12, 2017—I remember exactly that date—the CRC, the university's collegiate recovery community, accepted me. And they told me to go to the registrar with my letter of acceptance from them, and that would admit me and override the university's rejection.

I didn't really believe that, but I went anyway. I showed the registrar's office my letter from the CRC, and the lady went to the back room and checked with someone. She came out and apologized to me, and I was immediately accepted into the university.

My Life Today

That was over four years ago. Today I am almost five years sober. I'm now a senior and almost ready to graduate. I went through all of college sober! I owe so much to the CRC. They welcomed me and helped me to form a new identity and to believe in myself.

I'm also grateful to Victor, and to others who have come into my life through recovery. In 2020, with the help of a silent partner who was inspired by my story, I purchased the sober-living home I'd been in, and we've expanded it from five beds to fifteen. We've paid off our debt and I'm its CEO. This will be a part of my career, along with work in the therapy field. I'm going to graduate school so I can get licensed to work in mental health.

An Extraordinary Destiny

If I look back at myself in 2017, I could never have imagined how my life could be today. It's one thousand times better! My daughter, Adylinn, is now almost ten. I get along well with her mom, and I'm a big part of her life. I'm expecting my second daughter soon and grateful for that new gift. I'm really active in recovery, attending many meetings a week, and sponsoring other young men.

As I grew up, my aspiration was to be the best menial farm worker I could be. But then I got into recovery and went to college, and saw people doing these extraordinary things, and now I know I can do them too.

Today I know who I am, and I see that I can achieve great things for myself and for others. I know, too, that I need to serve others to be a leader. We're all equal and we're all worthy.

Esteem Yourself

Victor's impact on Marc was profound. He had a vision: Marc could have a good life if he took the steps Victor laid out for him. This helped Marc to believe in *himself*. Sometimes it just takes one other person in our lives, someone who sees *all* of us, our goodness, our courage, our worthiness. We integrate that truth—the real truth—and become who we always were, before addiction took our choices away.

Now in recovery, many of the storytellers have affirmed their self-worth.

In Chapter One, we heard from Kira and her journey from hating herself to loving who she is today—the *good* person she is. Sophie, in Chapter Two, moved from pain to purpose and she loves her life today. Wyatt's story in Chapter Five describes his self-acceptance, and in Chapter Seven, Charlotte said she loves her *own* version of herself – not someone else's.

Self-Care is Good Stewardship of Your Greatest Gift

For those of us with SUDs, we need healthy ways to soothe ourselves. I sometimes say I went from a binkie to a wine bottle (not exactly the most flattering description). Acts of self-love, commonly called "self-care," need to be in our toolkits. There are many ways—physical, emotional and spiritual—that we can be good stewards of the greatest gift we're given: Our lives.

We can get our bodies moving with bike rides, or runs, or gym workouts, to keep us strong. Emotional care can range from taking a calming yoga class, to lighting candles, or sitting outside with our faces drenched in bright sunlight. Spiritual care might mean making art and giving it away to someone you love, going on nature treks where you feel transcendence, or sitting in meditation or prayer.

When you take care of yourself, this truth dawns like daybreak: You're worthy of every good thing. Just because you're *you*.

You Loving You

Befriend.
Be kind.
Become and embrace the whole true you, and
Believe.

THREE

Living Sober, Stepping Out

Chapter Nine

Graduating

Do no harm. Take no shit.
—Unknown

When we graduate from college or trade schools, or rehabs, or sober outpatient programs, the promise of an exciting new world awaits. The one thing that matters most is maintaining your recovery as your future unfolds.

This is why so many collegiate recovery programs encourage students to have additional recovery practices beyond the CRC. Sadie mentioned exactly that in Chapter Two.

In this final chapter from young storytellers, you'll meet two people. The first is Paul. Ten months after he graduated college, he got into recovery, but then his program faltered. Now he's back in, and everything is a whole lot better.

Paul's story, to me, represents our humanness. None of us are always "on" with recovery, especially with its emotional and spiritual dimensions, and that's okay. Now we have tools, and when we're ready again, we know where to go, and what to do.

The next storyteller in this chapter is Jordan, who got sober as a senior in college. Today, many years later, Jordan still works an active program of recovery.

Paul

Growing Up Entitled

SCAN TO LISTEN

Growing Up, Romancing Alcohol

In my neighborhood growing up, drinking was normal for my mom, dad, and their friends. I created this romanticized version of alcohol from watching them with their drinks.

I had my first drink at fourteen. I liked the release, and it helped me to connect more with people. By high school, drinking was ingrained, and when I went to college, I pretty much drank nonstop.

College was Thirteenth Grade

College was like thirteenth grade for me. A few times in public I was so blacked out I ended up in jail. First I thought it was funny. But then it happened two more times and it wasn't so funny.

I'd been using marijuana heavily in college too, but stopped toward the end of college because potential employers were drug testing. When I gave up pot, my drinking took off to new levels.

Somehow, I graduated. I'd just always felt entitled throughout college, like after I graduated I just expected to fall into a career through family connections and have an easy road from there.

My Body Rebels

Two months after I left college, I was doubled over in pain and had to go to the hospital. It was the most relentless pain I have ever felt in my life. I knew that I was dying. The doctor told me I had pancreatitis, and if I wanted to live any kind of healthy life, I had to stop drinking.

I went through eight months of misery, then went back to attempting to control my marijuana, attempting to control my drinking. I finally went to rehab, at this wilderness camp in Utah. My parents had given me an ultimatum, so I went. The biggest surprise to me was realizing, when I was there, that I was an alcoholic. That my life really was out of control.

After rehab, I wasn't ready to stay sober on my own, so I went to a sober-living community with other young men like me. I started working the Steps there (note to reader: Steps are the Twelve Steps of AA, or NA, or other "Twelve-Step" programs), and that was really helpful.

Not Quite Ready

When I left the sober-living community, I thought I was ready to be on my own, but I wasn't. Transitioning out was hard, and I relapsed and the pancreatitis came back with a vengeance. I had to be hospitalized for it, but I lied to everyone about why I was in the hospital so they wouldn't know I had relapsed.

After two months of living with that lie, I just couldn't do it anymore. I knew enough about my disease, and the Steps, to know I had to come clean to my friends and family. So I called each of them and told them the truth. That was really hard.

Stepping Up Sobriety

That was over five years ago. I haven't taken a drink in that time, but I've often felt off, like I was sober but not emotionally sober. I had stopped going to meetings, and my program of recovery had started lagging. Recently I've picked back up going to AA meetings again. I found this great meeting with young men like me, I have a new sponsor, and I've aggressively dived into the Steps again with him.

I'm starting a small business, a service business for those with special needs. I find more and more that trying to help others is the best medicine for my disease.

I hope to grow this business and to keep progressing with my sobriety. It was always there, I just lost it for a time.

Jordan

Living Two Lives, and One Moment of Clarity

SCAN TO LISTEN

Growing Up with a Promise Broken

I picked up my first drink at fifteen and felt I could breathe for the first time. As a kid, I promised myself I would never become an alcoholic because of what I had witnessed growing up. But as soon as I took that first sip I said to myself, *Oh, this is why my family drinks*. I blacked out that first night and had the worst hangover, since it was from champagne. Even with that I couldn't wait to do it again, and I just thought *I'll switch to tequila*.

Right away I knew my drinking was different from other peoples', but I didn't care. My mom had started going to AA about that time, and she'd have women's meetings in our living room, while I'd be back by myself in my bedroom drinking. I'd think what a bunch of losers they were.

The Dark Days of College

College was my darkest time. I felt extremely lonely even though I had boyfriends and was surrounded by people. On paper my life looked a 90210 show, so I couldn't understand why it felt so awful.

Then in college people started dying from alcohol poisoning, and I realized I drank as much as they did. And I was getting physically violent, which really scared me. I couldn't understand how my personality could change so drastically since I would never do violent things or say such mean things sober.

Still though, I didn't want to stop drinking. So I saw a therapist instead.

This disease is so powerful. People who don't have it can't often understand how it changes *everything* you are, when you're in its grips.

Getting Sober, Living Two Lives

On July 4 of my senior year of college, I was drunk and had a blackout in a bar. I came to in their bathroom, and I looked at myself in the mirror and said: "You're not this girl." I couldn't get that out of my mind the next few months. On October 11 of that year, I stopped drinking and started going to AA. But I continued smoking pot. I didn't want to let go of the lifestyle—the friends, the drama, my boyfriend.

So I tried to do it both ways, no drinking but still using. I didn't understand that any substance misuse is likely a symptom of our disease. I got that life lesson from my self-induced hell during that time.

I came clean with my sponsor in April of the following year and got honest, which probably saved my life. I got sober at twenty-one, and here I am in my thirties and still sober! Yay!

Useful and Happy

At twenty-three, I started out working as a case manager for teen mothers. I witnessed the pain fifteen-year-old mothers were going through because, to my horror, the majority were raped by either their father, mom's boyfriend, or at a gang initiation. My organization had a partnership with an early learning center, and I watched their babies blossom, which made the hard days all worth it.

Today I am still passionate about working with children, food-insecure families, and other issues that interest me. Some of my current company's clients include all-girls public middle and high schools, where we focus on body empowerment and mental health, and a hunger relief initiative for Title One school students and families. Title One applies to schools with high numbers of children from low-income families. I love that I can feel useful working on social issues that are important to me.

Working a Program of Recovery Today

I've always had sponsees, even in my early twenties, and that work has been a lifeline to not only help someone else, but also to gauge how far my recovery has come. We have to do a lot of growing up in our twenties, and doing it fully awake and in public can be hard. I'm so grateful I'm someone with time in recovery, who still loves going to meetings and sponsoring. These help me to enlarge my spiritual life, and to be of service.

The Laughter Stayed with Me

The laughter I heard from my mom and her friends when I was a teenager in my bedroom drinking, stayed with me all those dark years I was using. My mom never forced recovery on me, she just modeled it. Today, in my work and life, I try to model it too.

Recovery is a Living Practice

Paul and Jordan actively work their programs of sobriety, and their practices live right beside their jobs and their daily routines. There are many, many ways to keep practicing, which are sprinkled throughout this book. Charlotte makes time for meditation, prayer, and gratitude affirmations, and she steps up meetings when she feels unsettled. Marc plans to work in the substance misuse field.

Our buffet tables illustrate many ways we can maintain a sturdy foundation of sobriety, which makes everything else in our lives possible.

If my experience in all the meetings I've attended is any measure, there's one tool that seems particularly foundational. The one thing I hear, almost every time someone returns to using is, "I stopped seeing my sober friends", or "I stopped going to meetings". So pay attention to that.

For the disease of addiction and the practices of recovery, the operative word is "progress." Without steady practices, our disorder progresses. On the flip side, with active programs, our lives progress and we grow into our best, truest, most brilliant selves.

Recovery has taught me to never give up on it. It's a thrill ride of hope!

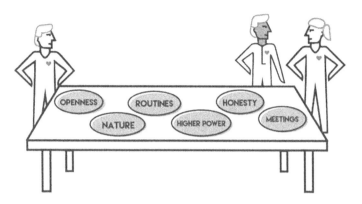

Illustration by *Elisa Vandergriff*

Even more buffet items on pages 34 and 45!

Chapter Ten

It's a Family Disease

A mother's love for her child is like nothing else in the world. It dares all things and crushes down remorselessly all that stands in its path.
–Agatha Christie

Data shows that one in three people in the US are impacted by substance use disorders. SUDs are wrenching on the families of the loved ones. They don't recognize the person who is in the grips of the disease, and they often feel powerless as to how they can help.

Here's one mother who did.

A Mother's Story

I Gave My Daughter a Painful Choice

SCAN TO LISTEN

Shortly after my daughter turned 21, I had a conversation with her that no parent ever wants to have. We were in our home in Marin County, California, and it was after lunchtime. I had just pulled her out of bed.

My daughter slumped in her chair, looking nothing like the vibrant and curious young woman I had raised. Her hair fell, uncombed, across her face. She was wrapped in a dirty blanket and looked like she was homeless. She stared at me with eyes I did not recognize, those of a young person whose light—and spirit—had gone out.

I mustered all my courage. "I love you very much," I said, "but you can't live here." My daughter looked at me as if she didn't understand. You have two choices," I continued. "You can go to rehab, which I'll pay for, or you can find somewhere else to live."

Several minutes passed as I waited nervously. My daughter had endured some difficult experiences in her life and had turned to alcohol and drugs to cope. I knew she needed help. I was a single mother, raising my children mostly on my own, and I was her last stop. She had nowhere else to go. I was taking an enormous risk, turning her away from my home.

I was also going against my every instinct as a mother. All I wanted to do was hold my beautiful girl in my arms, run my hands through her hair—half of which had fallen out, from stress—and soothe her until she was better, like I did when she was younger.

I was terrified about which option she would choose. But I had been trying for several years to get her help, with no success, and I had another child in the home, who I had to protect from the erratic behavior that accompanied my daughter's addiction.

I gave her a list of four treatment centers that I had researched. Amazingly, she chose one. Within five days, she checked into a young adult program at a well-respected facility.

That was not the end, but the beginning. In residential treatment, she started the hard work of recovery, which she continues to this day. She now has more than six years of sobriety.

I write this to let you know I've been there. I get it. I know what it's like to wake at 3:00 a.m., wracked with worry and grief, and terrified that your child or loved one may be lying in a ditch somewhere or at an out-of-control party or... worse.

I also know that there is hope.

It's true that there are no guarantees in life. Addiction is a potentially fatal disease. It could end in death. It could end in prison. Your family's outcome may be different from mine. But I want you to know that you are not alone. That's the first step toward healing—not only for your loved one, but also for yourself.

Does your child have a problem?

One of the toughest parts of having a young adult with a substance use disorder (SUD) is that it's tough to tell what's normal drinking/drug use and what's addiction. College students and other young adults party *a lot*. When that drug and alcohol use descends into a substance use disorder, there's also a lot of secrecy, which means that we-the parents and caregivers-don't always know what's going on.

How do you know if it's addiction? I struggled to figure this out with my daughter, so I know how tough it can be to make that call. But there are few things to watch for, such as your child engaging in secretive behavior, developing new struggles at school or work, getting into trouble with the law, experiencing money problems, or making excuses for why they couldn't show up for events or work or class. You may also smell smoke or alcohol on their breath, or there may be track marks on their arms, which often look like discoloration around a vein that's been bruised by injection.

Your child might insist that he or she is okay—and they probably believe this. When people suffer from addiction, they often don't see that they're sick and insist that they're "just having a good time." This is beyond frustrating to those of us who love someone who needs help, but it's also part of the disease.

The temptation is to take your loved one at their word and hope that the problem will go away. It may. But it may not. So, pay attention. It can be very painful to face the reality that someone you love is addicted, but it's a crucial first step.

I also urge you to get help from a professional, such as a doctor, therapist, addiction expert or intervention specialist. It's important to find someone who has received training in addiction education and counseling, and knows how to approach the problem (there's a lot of misinformation about addiction, including in the medical community). I relied on several professionals to guide me as I tried to help my daughter. This included a therapist and an intervention specialist, both of whom coached me on how to speak with my daughter and protect myself. We are not a wealthy family, but we had top-tier insurance at the time, which helped defray the costs. Still, I felt like I would spend my every last penny if it would keep my daughter alive.

My advice to you is: Keep going. As a parent or caregiver, you may be the person in the best position to get your child much-needed help.

Set appropriate boundaries

Living with—or loving—someone who is in the throes of an active substance use disorder is exhausting, and can have a profound effect on your physical, emotional, and financial health. To protect yourself and stay healthy, you need to set boundaries.

There is often confusion about what boundaries mean. Sometimes, people think that a boundary is a way to control another person's behavior. It's not. When we set a boundary, we're stating what is or is not okay with *us*.

When my daughter was in active addiction, we had an incident in which she took my car (without asking) and drove it while inebriated. I set a boundary that she wasn't allowed to have the keys to my car for thirty days. There was no way I was going to let her to use my car when I couldn't trust she'd be sober to drive it. I wanted to keep her—and all the other people on the road—safe. But also, it was my car and I needed it.

She was furious with me, and the upshot was that I had to drive her to all her appointments for a month. Trust me when I tell you that was not fun. But I set a boundary and stuck to it, and she took me seriously when I set other limits, later.

It's not your fault

It's important for you to understand that your child's addiction is *not your fault*. This comes as an enormous relief to most of us. At Twelve Step meetings for families, people often refer to the "Three C's:" We didn't *cause* the addiction, we can't *control* it, and we can't *cure* it. Sure, there are probably ways that you weren't a perfect parent or caregiver. None of us are. There are always things that we wish could have done differently. But substance use disorders can develop for a variety of reasons, including a genetic predisposition, mental health issues, or trauma (some of which you may not even know about, or had no ability to prevent).

Addiction can manifest in all sorts of families, including happy, healthy ones. Beating yourself up for your child's illness doesn't help anyone. So, be kind to yourself. You're dealing with enough tough stuff already.

Understand that recovery is not a quick or linear process

We were fortunate that my daughter did not relapse, but please understand: If your child or loved one relapses, that is part of the disease for many people. I have seen, among friends, how disappointing and heartbreaking it is when a kid relapses. But that does not mean that your child failed at treatment or will never recover. As with other chronic diseases, successful treatment for addiction requires continual evaluation and modification to keep a patient on track. This may mean that they need to go back to treatment or recommit to recovery meetings, or find a sponsor or a new approach with their medical team. It's very important to support them in the process and to share your understanding that relapse happens, which will help lessen your loved one's shame and stigma that often accompany relapse.

Know that recovery is a miracle

I remember the first time I saw my daughter at her aftercare program. I was with my other child, who nudged me and said, "Mom, look, the light is back in her eyes." And it was. After all the hell my daughter had gone through, suddenly there she was, back again. Since that time, she has occasionally asked me how she could make up for the difficulties her addiction caused. I always say, "I have what I want. I have my daughter back."

I have also always made it a point to let my daughter know that I believe she is an amazing and courageous person. When people first start in Twelve Step programs like AA and NA, they're often urged to look at all the ways they've messed up or caused harm. When my daughter would mention these to me, I would say, "Sweetheart, you can think whatever you want about yourself. But I also want to reflect back all the beauty and light I see in you now." We don't need to make our kids feel bad about themselves for being a struggling human, like everyone else on this planet.

Our kids are miracles. Recovery is a miracle. And you are a miracle because you care enough about someone to be reading this.

Epilogue

By telling our stories we become visible. We find our voices and discover all that's true about ourselves.

Our stories help us to connect, build our communities, and belong to one another. I listen to yours, then you to mine, and we feel less alone.

Thank you, Danni, Kira, Sophie, Sadie, Ahmed, Ted, Wyatt, Charlotte, Marc, Paul, Jordan, and "Mom," for being willing to share your stories. Maybe someone struggling today will hear yours, and they will be less afraid. We all get scared sometimes, but we're less scared together.

You are courageous. Lit bright. And now, in recovery, you are a light by which others can see.

Acknowledgements

Thank you, Danni, Kira, Sophie, Sadie, Ahmed, Ted, Wyatt, Charlotte, Marc, Paul and Jordan, as well as our mother in Chapter Ten, for being open and vulnerable enough to share your stories. You light the way for others coming after you, seeking experience and hope.

Thanks to the students and others who helped me to name this book, including Dawn, Charlotte, Kira, Wyatt, Olivia, Ted, Adrienne, Kristina, Ahmed, and probably some I've left out.

Thanks to ARHE's Kristina Canfield, whose passion for her work reinforced why this book was needed. Also to ARHE's Alexander Ronzino and SAFE Project's Jeff Horwitz and Kimberly Boulden.

For all the university staff and friends who helped me– Dawn Kepler, whose partnership allowed me generous access to her recovery students, and who helped me to think through parts of this book. To university supporters and resource providers – Lisa Parker, Anne Shoup, Chris Anthony and Dr. Cara Poland, Jen Cervi, Alee Trevino, George Comiskey, Teresa Herzog, and Matt Statman, Jennifer Tourville, Nathan Payne, Sarah McCall, and

Moira Binder. For Dr. Sam Stanley, president, MSU– by inviting me to give a commencement address, he helped spark the beginnings of this book.

To the "Tom's," Tom Nahas and Tom Lehner, along with Kelly Nahas, who made the stories come to life with audio. To Mario Nanos of FAN, whose passion for recovery is contagious. To my agent Joy Tutela, who urged me to write the little book *now* regardless of format, because the topic needing writing about. Thanks to my editors Mitra Malek and Adrienne Hand, and for Laura Hilgers, journalist extraordinaire, who kept asking the bigger questions. For Jane Tabachnick and team, whose expertise got this little book produced. And to Ahmed Hosni and Adrienne Hand for their wisdom along the way.

Thanks to my mighty team: Hannah Gils, director, social media ("Take more pictures Susan!"), and Elisa Vandergriff, director of design. Every winter she works patiently with me on materials for the next ARHE Conference, and 25 iterations later, she breathes a sigh of relief. Thanks to Antonella Iannarino, for her strategic brain and rebuilding of my online presence. And thanks to Joyce Ortiz, director, Susan's sanity. She's too polite to say she really doesn't want the job.

For Greg Boyle, my wisdom teacher. I keep shamelessly stealing his words because his writing is poetry.

And for Table 15. You know who you are.

Resources and Contact

If you'd like more information about SUDs, you can go to the SAMHSA site.

www.SAMHSA.gov.

For more information on college recovery, go to:

ARHE: https://collegiaterecovery.org

Or

SAFE Project: www.safeproject.us

If you're a caregiver, the mother from Chapter Ten recommends www.Shatterproof.org as a great resource.

If you're a graduate who wants to stay connected with other graduates in recovery, SAFE Project has created an app called ReconnectED. For more information, go to: www.safeproject.us/campuses/reconnected/.

Books, for students:

Voices of Recovery from the Campus: Stories of and by College Students in Recovery from Addiction, by Lisa Laitman, Dr. Linda Costigan Lederman and Irene Silos, 2015

Books, for community and university administrators:

Substance Abuse Recovery in College: Community Supported Abstinence, by Harrington Cleveland, Kitty S. Harris, Richard P. Wiebe, 2010

If you'd like to contact any of the storytellers, send me a message at www.hoperich.org

I promise I'll reply.

Susan

: Susan Packard
www.facebook.com/PackardSusan

: @SusanPackard
www.instagram.com/susanpackard/

: @PackardSusan
www.twitter.com/PackardSusan

: Susan Packard
www.youtube.com/channel/UCr-tihWzqigcOida7YJrLBg

: Susan Packard
www.linkedin.com/in/packardsusan

To reach Susan via her websites:
www.susanpackard.com
or
www.hoperich.org

Discussion and Study Guide

Abandonment: pages 49, 55

Acceptance (of having SUDs): pages 29, 52, 90, 93, 95, 98, 109

Adderall: pages 37, 60-64, 71

Adult's positive influence/ Champions: pages 51-54, 55, 99, 115

Adverse childhood experiences/ACEs: page 55

Belonging: all of Chapter Six–pages 78-85, plus 22-23, 63, 113

Blackouts: pages 21, 27, 62, 108, 112

Body/mental health connection: pages 91, 109

Buddhism: page 32

Careers supporting others: pages 22, 38, 53-54, 100, 111, 114-115

College Admissions: page 99

College Crash: page 39

Co-occurring mental health disorders: pages 26, 27, 41, 58-64

Disconnected/soul sick: pages 18, 21, 69, 78, 89, 113

Disease progression: pages 41-42, 51, 71, 82, 89, 98, 109, 113

Emotional Sobriety: 44, 103, 110, plus Buffet Tables– pages 34, 45, 117.

Escalation of SUDs in college; breaking the pattern: page 39

Family: "normal" upbringing: pages 57, 70, 88

Fears: pages 39, 44, 55

Felony: pages 22, 51

Fraternity for the Sunlight of the Spirit: page 53

Genetics: pages 18-19, 20, 27, 36, 71, 112

Goodness: pages 24, 33, 49, 68, 76, 87, 102-103

Gratitude: pages 74, 83, 91

Hitting bottom: pages 29, 52, 62-63, 71-72, 90, 98, 114

Honesty: all of Chapter Seven–pages 86-95, plus 16, 29, 52, 110, 114

Hope: pages 33, 44-45, 83, 116, plus See Recovery Practices

Integrity: page 95

Isolation: pages 24, 74

Meditation: pages 32, 45, 91

Pancreatitis: page 109

Parental tough love: pages 29, 37, 72, 88, 109, 119

Perfectionism: pages 21, 37, 88, 92, 93

Rape: pages 21, 37, 82

Recovery practices: within each Story, plus see Buffet Tables– pages 34, 45, 117.

Rehabs: pages 29-30, 52, 55, 61, 72, 89, 99, 106, 109

Relapse/return to use: pages 20-21, 42, 61-63, 89, 110

Resilience: page 33

Safety-physical, emotional: pages 44, 85

Self-Care: pages 102-103

Sober housing: pages 38, 63, 73

Soul sick: See Disconnected

Spiritual Sobriety: all of Chapter Five–pages 68-77, plus 16, 32, 83, 91, 98, 103, 115

Suicidal attempts/thoughts: pages 28, 62, 63, 72, 75

Tiptoeing out after getting sober: pages 30, 72, 90

Traumas*: pages 21, 28, 37, 42, 50-51, 55, 60, 71, 82

Twelve Step practices/ Higher Power: pages 12, 32, 42, 52, 63, 74, 98, 99, 110, 112-115

Unconditional love: page 49

Wholeness: page 95

Worth/Self -Worth: the last page of each Story, plus 87, 96, 102-104

---

* Not being a therapist, I used Michaelquirke.com 10 ACEs of Trauma to evaluate and include here.